TUNNELS

TUNNELS

Philip Sauvain

GEC **GARRETT EDUCATIONAL CORPORATION**

Edited by Rebecca Stefoff

U.S.A. text © 1990 by Garrett Educational Corporation
First Published in the United States in 1990 by
Garrett Educational Corporation, 130 East 13th Street,
Ada, OK 74820

First Published 1989 by Macmillan Children's Books,
England, © Macmillan Publishers Limited 1989

Manufactured in the United States of America

Library of Congress Cataloging-in-Publication Data

Sauvain, Philip Arthur.
    Tunnels / Philip Sauvain.
    p. cm. - (How we build)
    Includes index.
    Summary: Describes different types of tunnels and how they are made.
    ISBN 0-944483-79-8
    1. Tunnels-Juvenile literature. 2. Tunneling-Juvenile literature.
[1. Tunnels. 2. Tunneling.] I. Title. II. Series.
TA807.S28   1990
624.1'93-dc20
                                     90-40248
                                           CIP
                                             AC

Note to the reader
In this book there are some words in the text which are printed in **bold** type.
This shows that the word is listed in the glossary on page 46. The glossary
gives a brief explanation of words that may be new to you.

Contents

Why build tunnels?

What would we do without tunnels? Tunnels let us travel under cities, beneath rivers, and through mountains. Journeys that were once long, difficult, and dangerous have been made safer and shorter because tunnels have reduced the distance and time spent reaching destinations. There are also the tunnels we take for granted, like those that bring electricity, gas, and water into our homes and dispose of our sewage.

A simple job?

Building a tunnel might seem like a simple job. However, builders may find rock that is very hard to dig through, or rock that is so soft that the roof and sides of the tunnel start to fall in. In wet areas tunnels may fill up with water. Ways of transporting the rubble to the surface have to be considered when building long tunnels. Also, the tunnel may not run in a straight line. Yet when builders build from both ends of the tunnel, they have to make sure they will meet in the middle. Building a tunnel is not as simple as it looks.

Through mountains

Tunnels are built because it is cheaper and easier to drive a car or train through a mountain or under a river than it is to drive over or around it. A tunnel cut through a mountain is usually built on the level, so trucks and trains carrying goods and passengers can move faster than they can on steep mountain slopes.

Another advantage is that, unlike surface roads and railway tracks, a tunnel does not get blocked by snow in the winter.

A tunnel under a busy harbor or river keeps traffic moving more smoothly than waiting for a ferry to take it across. When trains travel in underground tunnels, they greatly reduce the traffic problems above. Imagine what would happen in cities if all the people who normally travel by underground subway or train traveled by car instead!

▶ The French entrance to the Channel Tunnel soon after drilling had started in 1988. Very large drilling machines were specially built to tunnel through the soft chalk under the English Channel.

▼ Mountain peaks and icy glaciers form a natural barrier between France and Italy. Today, the Mont Blanc Road Tunnel carries travelers through the Alps quickly and safely.

▼ Look at this map. If one inch (one centimeter) represents one mile (one kilometer), how far would you travel if you went along the long, winding railway line from Town A to Port B?

▼ Look at the same area after two tunnels were built. Using the same scale as before, measure how much shorter the distance is now between Town A and Port B.

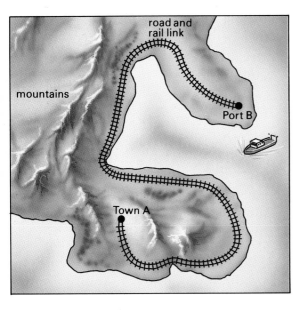

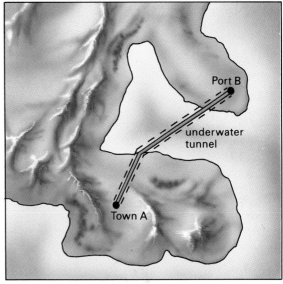

Long ago

Some of the earliest tunnels were built 4000 years ago, when people in Europe used deer antlers to dig pits and tunnels in search of pieces of flint to use for their simple tools and axes. At about the same time, Egyptian slaves were digging passages under the pyramids to construct the secret, treasure-filled burial chambers of the kings. The Egyptians used copper saws to cut through rock. They also used drills made from hollow reeds coated with powder from an **emery stone.** These tools would drill holes in the rock when they were turned rapidly. The Romans later built tunnels in many cities. A rock tunnel they built in Jerusalem is still in use today.

Roman engineers

The people who build roads, bridges, dams, and tunnels are known as **engineers.** Two thousand years ago, Roman engineers were bringing water into their cities through tunnels and constructing sewers under the streets of

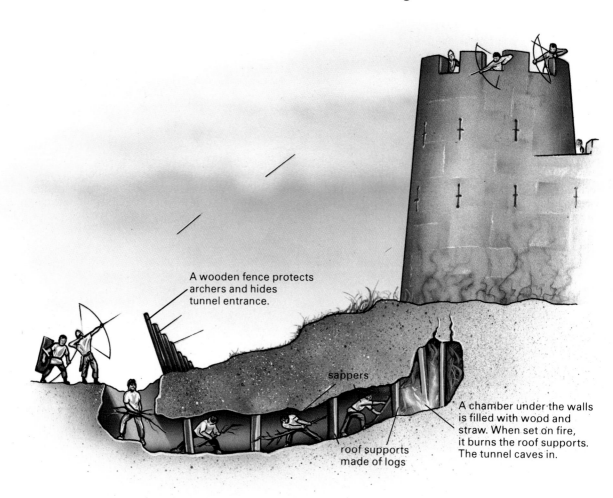

A wooden fence protects archers and hides tunnel entrance.

sappers

roof supports made of logs

A chamber under the walls is filled with wood and straw. When set on fire, it burns the roof supports. The tunnel caves in.

Rome. The Romans found ways of tunneling through solid rock by heating it with fire and then cooling it with cold water to break it up. One Roman general built the first known road tunnel near Naples in 36 BC. Holes or **shafts** were dug down to the tunnel from above to let in fresh air.

Tunnels in warfare

During the Middle Ages, soldiers in Europe often dug tunnels in order to gain entry to the fortified towns or castles of their enemies. These tunnels were called saps, and the soldiers who built them were called sappers. The sappers started the tunnel from their own camp and dug in the direction of the town or castle walls, propping up the tunnel roof with wooden posts as they went.

When the sappers judged that they had reached a point directly under the walls, they filled the end of the tunnel with straw. Then they set fire to the straw and ran back along the tunnel to safety. The flames burned the posts and, if they were lucky, the roof of the tunnel collapsed and brought down the walls above. The army behind them stood ready to charge through the ruined walls and capture the enemy stronghold.

Tunnels in mines

By the 1500s, people in Europe were beginning to dig tunnels into hillsides to mine coal and metals. These shallow, horizontal tunnels were called adit mines. In constructing an adit mine, the biggest danger came from underground water flooding into the tunnel. Even today, drainage is always a problem whenever a tunnel is built.

◀ Sappers were soldiers who were experts at building tunnels. They would dig under the walls of enemy castles and make them collapse.

▲ German miners tunneling through rock about 400 years ago. The search for coal and metals made it necessary to dig longer and deeper tunnels.

The age of machines

Until the 1800s, the major means of transportation was by water. However, rivers did not always go where the goods were needed. Some canals were built, but the early canal builders only had picks and shovels. This made it difficult to cut through hills of hard rock.

Then, in 1660, some French engineers working on a canal found a method of tunneling through hard rock. They made holes in the rock and filled them with gunpowder. When the gunpowder was set off, the explosions broke up large pieces of rock, leaving a hole. Repeated explosions cut deeper and deeper into the rock.

During the 1700s and 1800s, many other canal tunnels were built using the same method. These were the years of the Industrial Revolution, and canals were needed to transport coal to the new factories that were being built everywhere.

The coming of the railway

In 1830, the world's first steam railway opened between Manchester and Liverpool in England. To get the tracks into Liverpool, engineers had to build a tunnel one and one-quarter miles (two kilometers) long. Soon more railways were being built across Europe and the United States. Tunnels were necessary, especially in hilly areas, as the trains could not climb steep slopes.

▼ A mechanical drill was used between 1861 and 1871 to cut the 22 mile (13.7 kilometer) long Mont Cenis Tunnel through the Alps between Italy and France.

Safer building methods

In 1875, engineers working on the Hoosac Railway Tunnel in the United States started to use dynamite instead of gunpowder to break up hard rock. They also used a new method of setting off explosions electrically. Until then engineers had to light long fuses that sometimes went out. Now an electric spark could travel along a wire to the explosive, igniting it instantly.

At this time, too, an Italian engineer named Germain Sommeiller used a power drill to cut the Mont Cenis Tunnel

▲ In 1888 a tunnel was built under the River Thames. It formed part of the London Underground railway.

in the Alps. The drill was driven by **compressed air.** As the air expands, its force provides the power to drill holes into hard rock. Power drills were mounted on special railway trucks called **drill carriages.**

In London, engineers invented a machine to cut safely through very soft ground. The machine had a **tunneling shield** to hold the tunnel roof up, giving workers time to build supports.

Types of tunnel

How a tunnel is built and what it is made of depend on where it is to be built and what it will be used for.

Underwater or underground

Underwater tunnels can be built in two ways. Engineers may cut through the ground below the river as if they were constructing the tunnel under the land. The other alternative is to build a **sunken tube tunnel.** This is done by lowering large steel tubes onto the sea or river bed and joining, or **welding,** them together.

Usually tunnels run either underwater or underground. However, **cut-and-cover tunnels** are built differently. First the workers dig huge ditches, heaping the earth and rocks on either side. Then they use bricks, stones, or concrete to make the walls and roof of the tunnel. When it is finished, they cover it over with earth so that the land on top can be used again for farmland or for streets and buildings.

▶ Engineers calculate the exact position at which the tunneling team will break through. Their calculations are especially important if two teams are working toward each other from opposite ends. The sides of the two tunnels they cut should be less than 12 inches (30 centimeters) out of line with each other.

Building a tunnel with several shafts

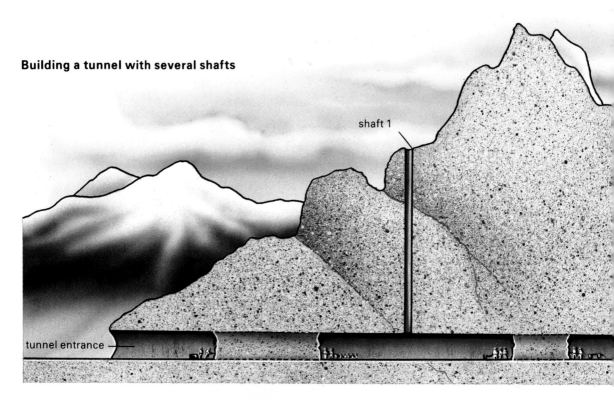

shaft 1

tunnel entrance

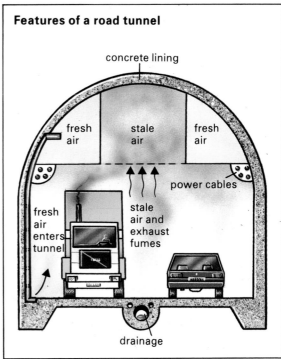

Features of a road tunnel

concrete lining

fresh air

stale air

fresh air

power cables

fresh air enters tunnel

stale air and exhaust fumes

drainage

▲ Tunnel designers must make sure that there is plenty of fresh air in the tunnel. The fresh air forces exhaust fumes and stale air out. Drains in the middle of the tunnel get rid of water that could cause flooding.

A single team of workers would take years to cut a tunnel through a mountain. Most long tunnels are built by two teams working from opposite ends. Sometimes shafts are sunk in the middle so that extra teams can speed up the work. Laser beams are used to line up the different sections of the tunnel.

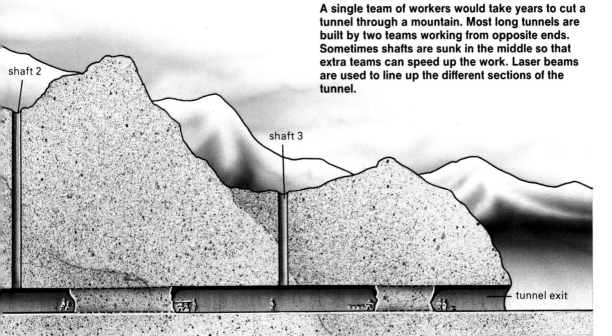

shaft 2

shaft 3

tunnel exit

Planning a tunnel

When engineers plan the route of a new road or railway, they must calculate whether it would be cheaper to build a road or a railway around a hill instead of cutting a tunnel through it. Even when the long route is cheaper to build, there may be good reasons for building a tunnel.

For example, tunnels often provide the shortest route from one place to another and so they save time and fuel for the people who drive through them. When the Mont Blanc Road Tunnel between France and Italy was opened in 1962, it reduced the distance by road from Paris to Rome by 124 miles (200 kilometers). Drivers of cars and trucks are usually willing to pay a toll to travel through a road tunnel if it will save them time and fuel costs. Truck companies using a tunnel can deliver their goods in less time, and drivers and passengers have a less tiring journey.

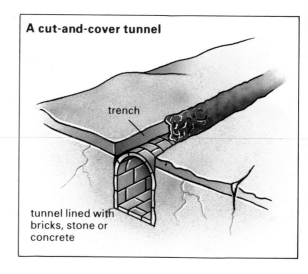

A cut-and-cover tunnel

trench

tunnel lined with bricks, stone or concrete

▲ The cut-and-cover tunnel is the simplest tunnel to build. It can be built only if all the buildings in its way can be pulled down.

Other considerations

Before a tunnel is built, engineers must calculate how much the tunnel will cost and how long it will take to build. They must know exactly where the tunnel will be dug and what kind of soil or rocks they will find there.

If different sections of the tunnel are to be built at the same time, the engineers must make sure that the sections will meet. They must try to foresee all the problems that may arise during the building of the tunnel. Will the workers be put at risk? Will blasting the rock with explosives endanger the public? Will the work interrupt traffic? How much road or rail traffic will pass through the tunnel when it is completed? What effect will that traffic have on homes, farms, or towns near the tunnel?

Size and shape

The purpose of the tunnel will usually determine its size and shape. Engineers try to keep the diameter of the tunnel as small as possible, because the larger the tunnel is, the greater the pressure of earth, rock, or water upon it will be. Tunnels for carrying sewage are often small and narrow. Road tunnels have to be high enough to take the largest vehicles on the roads, and may also have to be wide enough for several lanes of traffic.

▶ San Francisco has a modern underground railway system. It is called BART, the Bay Area Rapid Transit system, and crosses San Francisco bay through this sunken tube tunnel.

A bored tunnel

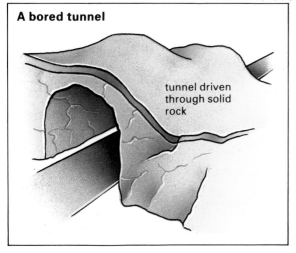

tunnel driven through solid rock

A sunken tube tunnel

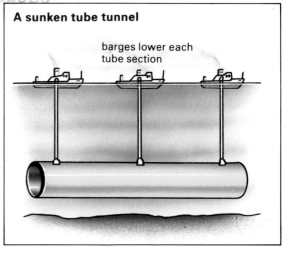

barges lower each tube section

▲ Most tunnels are cut through the ground. Engineers use explosives if it is hard rock and cutting machines if it is softer rock.

▲ Sunken tube tunnels are built instead of bridges. They can cross short stretches of water that are regularly used by shipping.

Testing the ground

Before engineers start to dig a tunnel, they find out as much as they can about the rocks on the site where it is to be built. They work with **geologists,** who are experts on the composition of the earth. The geologists drill **boreholes** into the ground along the route of the tunnel in order to obtain samples of the various types of rock.

▲ Before work begins on building a tunnel under the sea, samples of rock are taken from the sea bed. Samples were taken from beneath the English Channel before work was started on the Channel Tunnel between Britain and France. The samples showed that the sea bed was made up of soft rock.

Sampling the rock

The boreholes are made by **drilling rigs,** which support a long pipe. Attached to the end of the pipe is a **drillbit,** which is studded with diamonds, the hardest natural substance known. Machinery in the drilling rig rotates the pipe, so that the drillbit bores into the rock. As the borehole becomes deeper, extra pipes are added from the rig. These collect earth and rock.

If the rock samples are from hard rock, the engineers will blast through it by drilling holes and using explosives. If the rock samples are softer, they may use **tunnel-boring machines.** If the ground is very soft, they will probably use a tunneling shield.

Layers of rock

By studying the samples, geologists can tell the engineers if the rocks have been changed in any way by movements of the earth's surface over the ages. Layers of rock are sometimes folded back on themselves, a feature which geologists call a **fold.** Sometimes the movements of the earth's surface caused giant cracks, called **faults.** There the sides of the crack have shifted and the rock has broken up and fallen down in between. Tunnel workers cannot drill into these shattered rocks. They have to treat them with great care. They know that there may be water trapped inside that could flood the tunnel. Japanese workers came across a fault like this when they dug the Shin Kanmon Railway Tunnel between Japan's main island of Honshu and the southern island of Kyushu. It took three months to cut a section of tunnel only about 100 feet (30 meters) long across the fault.

Testing earth samples

You will need: a coin and some samples of earth and rock, such as a stone, an old brick, a lump of clay, and a piece of coal.

1 Scratch each sample with your fingernail. Can you see the scratch?

2 If not, try to scratch it with the coin. Can you see a scratch now?

3 The sample is soft if you can make a scratch in it with your fingernail. Workers cannot drill a tunnel in ground as soft as this. They have to use cutting machines.

4 If you cannot scratch the sample with the coin, then it is hard. Workers have to use explosives to drive a tunnel through rock as hard as this.

stone

coin

brick

clay

coal

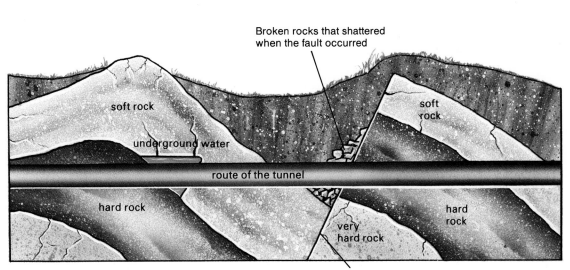

Broken rocks that shattered when the fault occurred

soft rock

soft rock

underground water

route of the tunnel

hard rock

hard rock

very hard rock

These rocks are folded over. This is an upfold, because the rocks are folded upwards.

This is a fault. The rocks on the left have broken away and slipped down.

A team cutting a tunnel through these rocks would find the tunneling difficult, although the engineers will be aware of the problems from the geologists' tests.

Solving the problems

Tunnel builders know that every tunnel they construct will have its own set of problems to be solved. If the rock is very hard, it will take a long time to cut the tunnel through the ground. If the rock is soft, it will be necessary to support the roof and sides of the tunnel immediately, or they will fall in.

The job of the engineer is especially difficult if there is a mixture of hard and soft rocks in the tunnel. The machines used for cutting hard rock are not the same as those used for cutting soft earth. Cutting a tunnel through different types of rock is so complicated that the engineers may choose another route for the tunnel instead.

▼ These underground caves are in Morocco. Over the ages, some of the rocks have been worn away by water. Other, harder rocks have stood firm.

Shaping the tunnel

You will need: a tube made out of strong cardboard, a ruler, water, and a few cupfuls of dry sand.

1 Heap the dry sand in a pile. Try to dig a tunnel through to the other side. Then add water to make the sad wet. Try to dig the tunnel again. What do you notice?

2 Shape the roof and sides of the tunnel with the ruler to make them square. Press down on the sand until the tunnel falls in. Did you have to press hard?

3 Reshape the sand with the tube so that the tunnel is round. Do the test again.

4 Which is stronger, the square-shaped tunnel or the tube-shaped one?

sand

cardboard tube

Supporting the roof

Before the engineers start to cut a tunnel, they work out the **stand-up time** of the rocks through which the tunnel will be cut. This is the length of time that the roof and sides can stand up on their own without support.

If a tunnel is cut into loose, dry sand, the stand-up time may be only a second or two. If a tunnel is cut into clay, the stand-up time may be several minutes or even several hours. Very hard rock, such as granite, can stand without support for thousands of years unless it is exposed to wind, heat, or water.

The stand-up time of a tunnel also depends partly on its shape. Most tunnels have roofs shaped like an arch or a tube. A round arch is much stronger than a square or pointed roof, making the stand-up time of a tunnel longer.

Even after a tunnel is built, it may need a **lining** to support the roof. This lining, which may be a layer of cement, stone, brick, or metal, prevents soil and rock from falling into the tunnel.

Through hard rock

When engineers start to cut a tunnel through hard rock, the first thing they have to do is drill small holes in the rock. These holes will be filled with explosives powerful enough to blast a large hole right through the rock. This hole will eventually become the tunnel.

Drilling and blasting

Tunnel workers use a huge drill carriage called a **jumbo** to drill the holes for the explosives. The jumbo is divided into sections so that several workers can work on it at the same time. Attached to the front are power drills that bore holes in the rock. The drillbits are tipped with hard metal, but they get worn down and have to be changed from time to time.

The jumbo's drills make a lot of dust as they bore through the rock. Some drills are fitted with hoses, so that water spurts out through holes in the top, turning the dust into mud, which collects on the ground. This keeps the dust from getting into the eyes of the workers.

▼ This jumbo is mounted on rails. Its power drills are attached to two long booms.

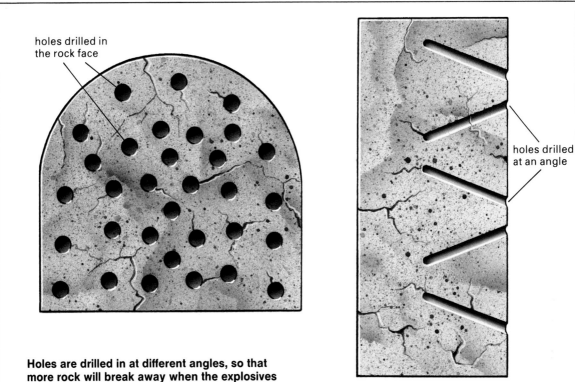

holes drilled in the rock face

holes drilled at an angle

Holes are drilled in at different angles, so that more rock will break away when the explosives go off.

Drilling patterns

The holes are drilled into the rock at different angles and in specific patterns. Engineers found out long ago that holes drilled into rock at an angle caused the explosives to break up more rock than holes that are drilled straight in. Each hole is about two and one-third inches (six centimeters) wide. The workers drill the holes about 16 to 20 feet (5 or 6 meters) deep. There may be as many as 200 holes in a single rock face.

Blowing up the rock face

When all the holes have been drilled, the engineers put sticks of explosives inside and wire them up to the electric **detonator** that will set them off. Using electricity, they can set off several explosions within a few seconds of each other. Tunnel workers have to be very careful when using powerful explosives. They need to know exactly how much of the explosive to use and how to use it safely.

The first explosions break off pieces of rock in the middle of the rock face and make a large hole. The next explosions are timed so that the pieces of rock that break off fall into the hole already blasted. With just one series of explosions, the engineers are able to cut away a complete slab of rock of the height and width needed for the tunnel.

Clearing the rubble

The workers have to wait until the smoke and fumes caused by the explosions have cleared away before they can enter the tunnel. Then, as soon as it is safe, they begin removing the broken rock. In some tunnels, **front-end loaders** and trucks are used to move the rock away. In other tunnels, it is loaded onto **conveyor belts** for removal.

As soon as the rubble is removed, the work of supporting the roof in that section of the tunnel begins. Not all rock tunnels need support, but even when the rock is hard, the tunnel workers often have to line the roof with steel mesh, held in place by **roof bolts.** The bolts are driven through the steel mesh into the solid rock, so that any loose earth or rock is contained by the mesh.

If the rock is cracked or broken, or if water starts to come through, it may be necessary to line the tunnel with concrete. Once this is done, the workers can move the jumbo into place in front of the new, deeper rock face. There, they begin all over again, drilling holes for the explosives that will open up the next stretch of tunnel.

▼ Front-end loaders may be used to scoop up the tons of broken rock that have been blasted from the rock face. When the way forward is cleared and made safe, the next section of the tunnel can be dynamited.

▲ A worker puts a roof bolt in the tunnel workings. Roof bolts prevent rock from falling into the tunnel while the work continues.

▼ One of the easiest ways to remove soil or rocks during tunneling is to use a conveyor belt. The belt carries the rubble away from the rock face, where it can be loaded onto trucks.

Inside the tunnel

Inside the tunnel, working conditions get very tough. No longer are the tunnel workers operating in fresh air and daylight. They have to work by artificial light, and dust, smoke, and fumes get into their eyes, nose, and mouth. There is the constant whining, grinding sound of power drills, as well as the deafening noise which is heard at the site whenever there is an explosion. Because of the noise level, tunnel workers often wear earplugs to protect their ears. They communicate with each other by using hand signals.

As the workers push deeper into the tunnel, the work is hard, heavy, dirty, and dangerous, but it can be exciting. Neither the engineers nor the other workers ever know what problems they will have to face next.

Mountain tunnels

The problems of tunneling through rock are at their worst when the tunnel is built through a mountain or range of mountains. Yet tunnels are often badly needed in such places, because mountain roads become dangerous and can be completely blocked by snow.

The Simplon Tunnel

The Simplon Tunnel runs through the Alps between Brig in Switzerland and Iselle in Italy. It is one of the longest railway tunnels in the world, with a length of more than 12 miles (20 kilometers). The Simplon Tunnel is made up of two parallel tunnels with a railway track running through each one. One of the tunnels was originally a smaller pilot tunnel that was cut through the mountain to help in the work on the main tunnel. Later it was enlarged to take a railway.

At one point the tunnel is nearly 7000 feet (2100 meters) below the summit of the mountain. This caused problems for the engineers because the deeper they cut into the rock, the hotter it became. About five miles (eight kilometers) from the Swiss end, the temperature became so high that the rock had to be sprayed with ice-cold water. The water was pumped into the tunnel from cold springs to make the temperature bearable for work to

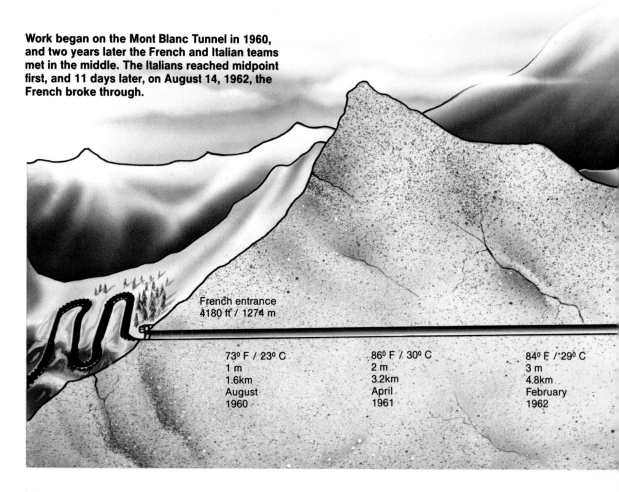

Work began on the Mont Blanc Tunnel in 1960, and two years later the French and Italian teams met in the middle. The Italians reached midpoint first, and 11 days later, on August 14, 1962, the French broke through.

French entrance
4180 ft / 1274 m

73º F / 23º C
1 m
1.6km
August
1960

86º F / 30º C
2 m
3.2km
April
1961

84º F / 29º C
3 m
4.8km
February
1962

continue. Hot springs and underground streams added to the workers' problems. One area of rock exerted such pressure on the structure that it took seven months to construct 138 feet (42 meters) of tunnel.

The Mont Blanc Tunnel

The Mont Blanc Tunnel is one of the longest road tunnels in the world. Motorists drive seven miles (11.25 kilometers) through the tunnel from France to Italy. As they do so, they pass beneath Europe's highest mountain, Mont Blanc, which is 15,770 feet (4807 meters) high.

The Mont Blanc Tunnel was blasted through solid rock by one French and one Italian team, each working from opposite ends of the mountain. In August 1962, when they met in the middle of the mountain, they found that their two sections of tunnel were less than eight inches (20 centimeters) out of line.

It took three years to cut the tunnel through Mont Blanc. During that time, the workers faced many difficulties. In one part of the tunnel, the temperature was 86° F (30° C). In another, under a glacier, it fell to minus 7° F (14° C). There were rock falls and, in some places, underground water trapped inside the rocks flooded into the tunnel. However, all these problems were solved, and the tunnel was opened to traffic in 1965.

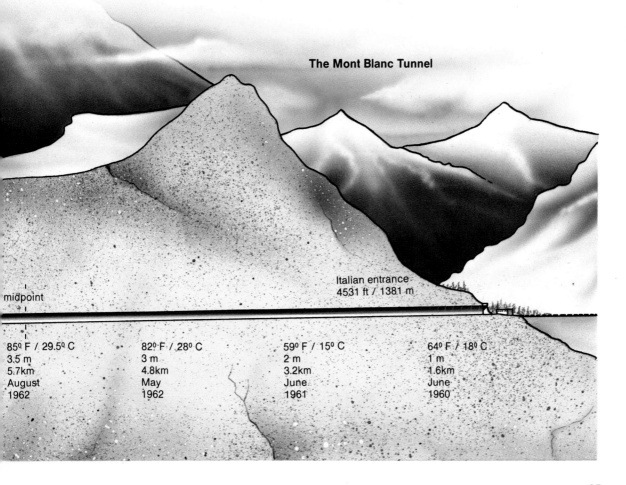

The Mont Blanc Tunnel

Italian entrance
4531 ft / 1381 m

midpoint

85° F / 29.5° C	82° F / 28° C	59° F / 15° C	64° F / 18° C
3.5 m	3 m	2 m	1 m
5.7km	4.8km	3.2km	1.6km
August	May	June	June
1962	1962	1961	1960

Tunneling through soft ground

Tunneling through soft ground is almost as difficult as cutting through the hard rock of a mountain. The use of the tunneling shield, however, makes the work easier and safer.

A tunneling shield performs two basic jobs. First, it protects the workers. The shield holds up the tunnel roof so that the people working inside it are not injured if the roof starts to crumble. Also, in some cases, the front part of the shield is filled with compressed air, which stops water from leaking into the tunnel.

At the same time, the tunneling shield is extending and shaping the tunnel. Pieces of equipment known as **hydraulic jacks** push the shield forward. As it moves, a sharp edge at the front of the shield cuts through the soft ground. While the machine digs, it also puts strong supports for the roof into place. Trucks take the loose earth away as the shield moves forward.

Very soft ground

Tunnel workers sometimes cut into ground that is too soft, or too full of water, even for a tunneling shield. The ground may be full of cracked or broken rock. The engineers then have to find a way of making the ground hard enough to cut into with their machines. Sometimes they fill the holes and cracks with a liquid cement called **grout.** When the grout sets, it makes the ground firm enough for the digging to go ahead.

If the ground is full of water, the

▲ The tunneling shield protects workers from roof falls as they dig through soft ground.

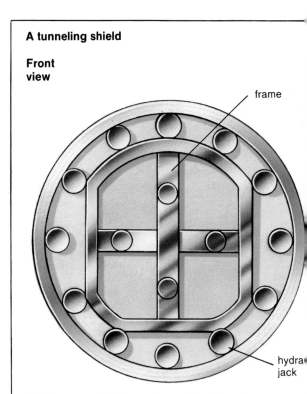

A tunneling shield

Front view

frame

hydraulic jack

Workers must go through an air lock as they pass into the front part of the shield, which is filled with compressed air. Compressed air stops water from leaking into the tunnel.

engineers may try to make it firm by freezing the water. They insert a system of long tubes filled with **liquid nitrogen** into the ground where the tunnel is to be dug. As the nitrogen circulates through the tubes, it freezes the water in the soil. The workers can then drive the tunnel forward through the frozen ground. Tunnels up to a mile (1.5 kilometers) long have been built using liquid nitrogen.

Lining the tunnel

A tunnel dug in soft ground has to be lined with concrete to prevent the roof and sides from crumbling away. The lining also prevents water from soaking into the tunnel. Some tunneling shields spread a concrete lining evenly over the tunnel as they move forward. If the tunnel sides are made of very loose earth or stones, however, the workers may have to use a machine that shoots liquid concrete in thin layers over the tunnel interior. This material is called **shotcrete.**

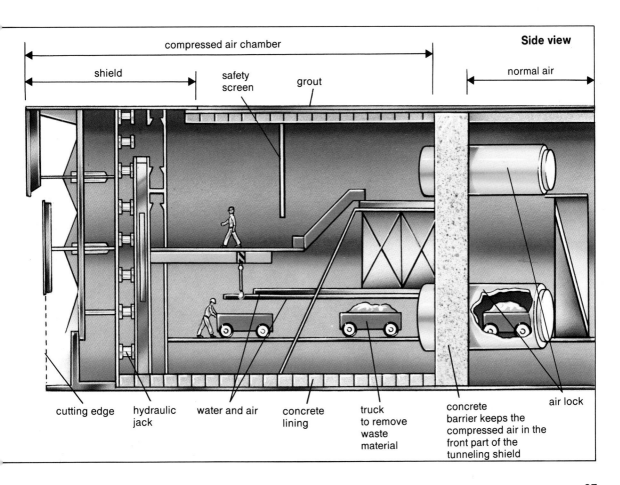

compressed air chamber

Side view

shield

safety screen

grout

normal air

cutting edge

hydraulic jack

water and air

concrete lining

truck to remove waste material

concrete barrier keeps the compressed air in the front part of the tunneling shield

air lock

Boring a tunnel

To cut through rocks that are not too soft and not too hard, tunnel builders use boring machines. Some of these machines are like giant power drills with sharp teeth that cut into the rock face as they rotate.

A tunnel-boring machine was invented over a hundred years ago by a British engineer named Colonel Frederick Beaumont, when plans were first being made to build a tunnel under the English Channel. In 1883, he demonstrated that his machine could cut a tunnel eight feet (two and a half meters) wide through chalk rock at a rate of 50 feet (15 meters) a day.

The Channel Tunnel was abandoned, and nothing more was heard about the tunnel-boring machine until 1954, when American engineers used a **rotary excavator** to dig a tunnel at the Oahe Dam on the Missouri River in the United States. The design of the rotary excavator they used was based on the tunnel-boring machine invented by Colonel Beaumont.

Tunnel-boring machines

Over a hundred years after Colonel Beaumont's plan to cut a tunnel beneath the English Channel, building work started on the British-French Channel Tunnel.

Special tunnel-boring machines were designed to cut the three long tunnels under the sea bed for the tunnel. Using these machines, the engineers estimated it would take only six years to complete the 30 mile (49.4 kilometer) tunnel.

Tunnel-boring machines have great advantages over blasting with explosives. Only a few workers are needed to manage them, and there are none of the risks that go with using explosives. Also, they can cut rapidly through softer rock. The only disadvantages of tunnel-boring machines are that they are expensive to buy, and they are not practical for tunneling through very hard rock.

Eating away the rock face

Tunnel-boring machines are sometimes called **mechanical moles.** The sharp teeth at the front of the machine tear strips off the rock face and leave grooves behind in the walls of the tunnel.

The biggest tunnel-boring machines can carve out a tunnel as wide as 36 feet (11 meters). A giant mechanical mole like this was used in recent years in Liverpool, in England, to cut a tunnel under the Mersey River.

◄ This tunnel-boring machine was invented by Colonel Beaumont over one hundred years ago, during an early attempt to build a Channel Tunnel. Compare it with the modern machine on the opposite page.

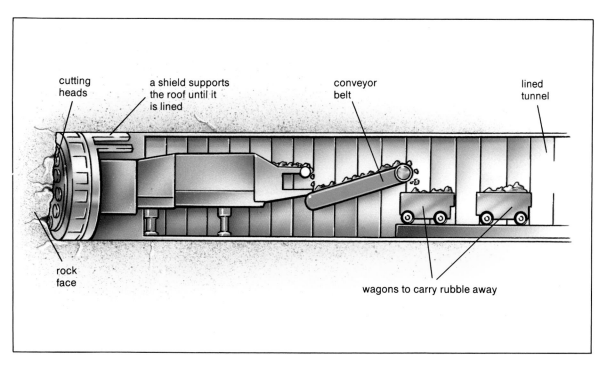

cutting
heads

a shield supports
the roof until it
is lined

conveyor
belt

lined
tunnel

rock
face

wagons to carry rubble away

▲ **The sharp teeth at the front of the tunnel-boring machine spin around at a high speed. They cut deeply into the rock.**

▼ **Engineers check a tunnel-boring machine. At the front is the large cutting head. Rubble is carried to the rear along a conveyor belt.**

Underwater tunnels

Tunnels under the water have many advantages over bridges. Tunnels are often cheaper to build, do not get in the way of passing ships, and are not affected by high winds, which can close a bridge to traffic . Tunnels can also cross deep areas of water, where it is difficult to build bridges.

The challenge

Building a tunnel under a river or beneath the sea is a great challenge to the engineers in charge of the project. The worst problem is water seeping into the tunnel through the ground above. For this reason, engineers often fill the tunnel with compressed air in order to keep out the water.

Engineers must also work out a way of ventilating the tunnel. They usually do this by blowing in air from each end of the tunnel, rather than through shafts from the surface.

Island to island

The most exciting tunnel projects of the twentieth century are the Seikan Tunnel in Japan and the Channel Tunnel between Britain and France. Both are underwater tunnels. At 33.5 miles (54 kilometers) long, the Seikan Tunnel in Japan is the world's longest railway tunnel. It was built to join the island of Hokkaido in the north of Japan to the main island of Honshu. Work began on it in 1946 and was only completed in 1988, 42 years later.

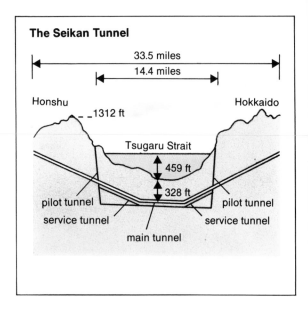

Island to mainland

The Channel Tunnel is also a railway tunnel, designed to link Britain to France and the rest of Europe. Eleven giant tunnel-boring machines were built to dig the tunnel through the chalky clay 164 feet (50 meters) below the sea bed. This soft rock is easy to bore through, so the machines are able to cut through the ground at a rate of six and one-half feet (two meters) per hour.

The Channel Tunnel is an enormous undertaking. Everything about it is impressive. The two main tunnels are 25 feet (7.6 meters) in diameter, while the service tunnel between is 16 feet (4.8 meters) in diameter. The engineers estimate the construction will take over eight million

▶ The design for the Channel Tunnel includes three tunnels. Two large tunnels carry trains between Britain and France. A smaller service tunnel runs between them, carrying cables for power and lighting and a water pipe in case of fire.

tons of cement and a quarter of a million tons of steel. Because of the pressure of the water above, the roof of the tunnel is supported by concrete and braced with cast-iron rings for extra strength.

When the Channel Tunnel is completed, it will cut the travel time between London and Paris in half. Train travelers, who at present must change to a ferry for the Channel crossing, which takes at least an

▲ The Seikan Tunnel is in Japan. Here, the drilling has been completed and the tunnel is being lined with steel and concrete.

hour and a half, will remain on their trains. Motorists, instead of boarding the car ferry, will drive their cars onto special shuttle trains. By rail through the tunnel, the crossing will take only 28 minutes.

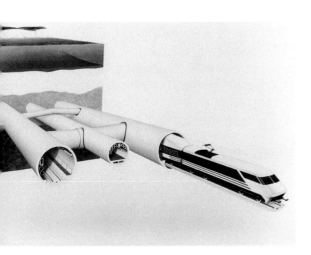

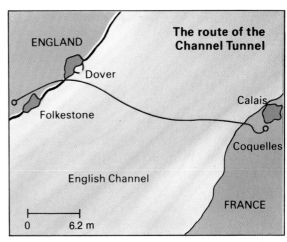

The route of the Channel Tunnel

ENGLAND

Dover

Folkestone

Calais

Coquelles

English Channel

FRANCE

0   6.2 m

Sunken tube tunnels

For some kinds of underwater tunnels, the work begins in a steel factory, where huge section of steel tubes are made. They may be as large as 328 feet (100 meters) long and 49 feet (15 meters) in diameter. These tubes will be sunk to the sea floor and welded together to form a tunnel. In the factory, both ends of each section of tube are blocked off by steel plates called **bulkheads,** trapping the air inside. This will make it possible to float the tubes to the tunnel location.

▲ Engineers lower a steel tube into a dredged channel. They protect the tube by covering it with sand and mud.

Laying the tube

Before the tubes can be laid in place, a deep channel has to be dug, or **dredged,** in the sea bed. Then tugs tow the tubes to the site, where they are gently lowered, one at a time, into the channel. Divers go down to check that the huge bolts on the end of each tube are slotted into holes in the sections of tube already lying in the trench. The join between the two tubes is later sealed with concrete. When all the tubes are in place, workers go inside the tubes and cut away the bulkheads separating the different sections and weld the edges together to make one long tunnel.

▼ Huge tubes being floated across Hong Kong's harbor during the construction of the Cross Harbor Tunnel. Engineers on the platform in the foreground will supervise, to make sure that the tubes are lowered into the correct position on the harbor floor.

Chesapeake Bay

The longest sunken tube tunnel in the world is the Bay Area Rapid Transit Tunnel in San Francisco in the United States. It is also called the BART tunnel.

Two sunken tube tunnels also form part of the causeway that stretches 17 miles (28 kilometers) across the mouth of Chesapeake Bay in the United States. They were constructed in 1964 so that large ships could enter the bay without having to pass under a bridge. The tunnels, nearly two miles (three kilometers) in length, are made up of 19 steel tubes, each weighing 12,000 tons. At the entrance and exit of each tunnel, artificial islands were built to link the tunnels to the rest of the causeway.

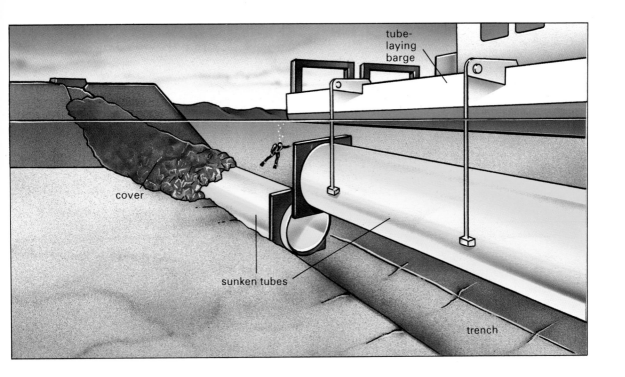

tube-
laying
barge

cover

sunken tubes

trench

Sinking a tunnel

You will need: some building blocks, several cardboard tubes, sticky tape, and a sink.

1 Join the ends of the tubes with tape to make a continuous tunnel. Then cover all but the ends of the tunnel with tape to make it waterproof.

2 Lay two rows of blocks at the bottom of a basin of water, leaving a gap the width of the tunnel between the rows.

3 Lower the tube tunnel into the sink so that it lies between the rows of blocks. Keep the ends above water. Cover the tunnel with other blocks to keep it from floating to the surface.

4 Prove that you have succeeded in making a sunken tube tunnel by blowing through the tubes!

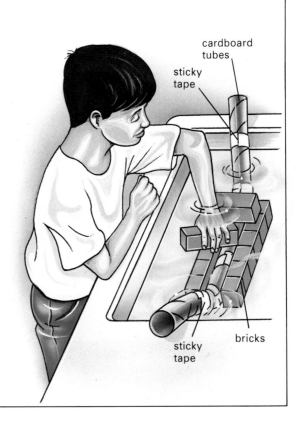

cardboard
tubes

sticky
tape

bricks

sticky
tape

Under the city

The oldest underground railway system in the world today is the London Underground. Parts of it were built over 125 years ago, excavated out of soft clay and gravel. In contrast, much of the 80-year-old New York City Subway was cut through solid rock.

The tracks for the first steam trains on the London Underground were laid in huge cut-and-cover tunnels following the course of the streets. In places they ran on the surface only a little way below street level. In 1890, however, the first deep-level section of underground railway was opened. One stretch of it went under the River Thames. The new line used electric locomotives instead of steam trains. The tunnel under the Thames was built with the aid of a tunneling shield using compressed air to stop water from leaking into the tunnel.

Many new underground systems have been opened in the last 20 or 30 years. Today, most of the world's major cities—including Washington DC, San Francisco, Moscow, Mexico City, and Hong Kong—have underground railways. Paris has had one, known at the Metro, since 1900. The streets of these cities are so crowded that it may take an hour to drive through the city center. Below the surface of the streets, however, an underground train can make the same journey in a few minutes.

Below the streets

Even cities that have no underground systems have an amazing number of tunnels under the streets, bringing

▲ A new sewage tunnel beneath the streets of London. Large cities need sewers in order to stay clean and healthy.

electricity, water, and gas into the city and taking away sewage. Engineers have to design each tunnel carefully to avoid breaking into one tunnel when they are digging another. For this reason, much of the London Underground is buried 80 to 90 feet (24 to 27 meters) below ground level.

The engineers also have to make sure that the tunnels they dig do not undermine the ground above. If earth sinks into the tunnel, the ground on the surface above it may gradually sink, too. This is called **settlement.** Settlement can cause cracks in buildings or even make them collapse.

Vibration from the trains is also a problem in cities like New York in the United States, where the underground railway lines are not far below ground level. It can shake the foundations of buildings and make life uncomfortable for the people who live or work in them.

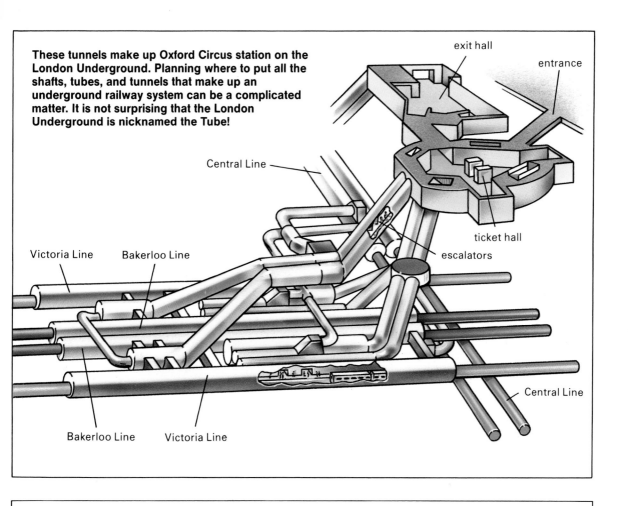

These tunnels make up Oxford Circus station on the London Underground. Planning where to put all the shafts, tubes, and tunnels that make up an underground railway system can be a complicated matter. It is not surprising that the London Underground is nicknamed the Tube!

exit hall

entrance

Central Line

Victoria Line

Bakerloo Line

ticket hall

escalators

Central Line

Bakerloo Line

Victoria Line

Laying tunnels

You will need: a large heap of sand, several drinking straws, and cardboard tubes of different sizes.

1 Make a model of tunnels under a major city. Start by putting the large tubes to carry the underground railway lines under the sand.

2 Choose drinking straws in different colors and sizes for the tunnels carrying sewage, waters, electricity, and gas. make sure these tunnels do not get in each other's way.

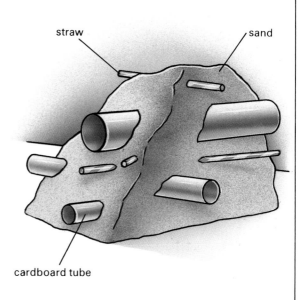

straw

sand

cardboard tube

Carrying water

Some tunnels have been built to carry water instead of traffic. The longest tunnel system in the world is in the United States. It takes water from the Pepacton and Rondout reservoirs in the Catskill Mountains to New York City. Completed in 1944, it is known as the Delaware **Aqueduct** system. Its tunnels, which are about 13 feet (4 meters) wide, cover a distance of more than 105 miles (169 kilometers).

Another long tunnel carrying water is the Orange-Fish Tunnel in South Africa, which is 51 miles (83 kilometers) in length. This tunnel is part of a huge irrigation system that carries water to fields in areas where there is little rain.

Power from water

Tunnels also carry water to **hydroelectric power stations,** which use water power to make electricity. Cut into the solid rock of a mountain, the tunnels bring water from a reservoir to the power station to drive the **turbines.** The power of the falling water makes the turbines spin around at high speed. A shaft transfers the circular motion of the turbines to a machine called a generator, which produces electricity.

Many of the world's largest power stations use tunnels to supply water to their turbines. Both the power station and the tunnels may be built inside a mountain. This avoids spoiling the surrounding countryside and also gives the tunnels

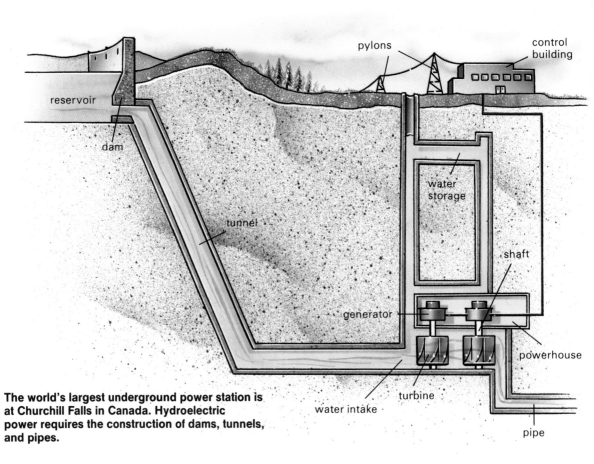

The world's largest underground power station is at Churchill Falls in Canada. Hydroelectric power requires the construction of dams, tunnels, and pipes.

enough strength to withstand the force of
the water as it thunders down to the
turbines.

▲ A huge tunnel over 32 feet (10 meters) wide being
built to carry water at high speed to the turbines at
Chute-de-Passes power station in Quebec, Canada.

Moving rivers

Tunnels are often used, together with dams,
to change the course of rivers. In British
Columbia, in Canada, a long tunnel was
cut through the rock of Mount Kemano to
the Nechako River. The river had been
dammed so that it created a reservoir and
also changed the course of the Nechako

River. The water from the reservoir is taken
through the tunnel into the hydroelectric
power station built inside the mountain.
The Kemano Power Station makes
electricity for use in the huge aluminum
works at Kitimat, by the Pacific
Ocean.

Safety in tunnels

Safety is a problem from the time the construction of a tunnel begins. Nearly 200 workers lost their lives when the St. Gotthard Rail Tunnel was cut through the Swiss Alps over a hundred years ago. In our own century, more than 30 Japanese workers died building the Seikan Tunnel.

Water

Water flooding into a tunnel is a major hazard and remains one even after the tunnel is completed. The danger of flooding is usually found to be greatest in underwater tunnels. Electric pumps are used to drain the water out when they are built and are kept ready to pump out water if it flows back in when the tunnels are in use.

Dust

Many types of rock give off clouds of fine dust when they are drilled. If the dust gets into the lungs of workers, it chokes them. Prolonged exposure to dust can cause lung disease or even death. For this reason, water is sprayed onto the rock face to stop the dust from flying around in the air.

▼ The lining of a tunnel being prepared in Bangkok, Thailand. The worker wears a hard hat to protect his head from falling masonry or machinery. He also wears a mask to protect his lungs from dust.

Sometimes water is made to pour over the rock in a continuous stream during drilling.

Heat

Temperatures deep inside the earth at the center of a tunnel can be very high. Part of one California tunnel was hotter than the Sahara Desert! Ice-cold water is sometimes sprayed on the rock face to cool it down. Refrigeration machinery has even been used in some tunnels to cool down the working area so that the workers can cut a tunnel through rocks heated by hot springs.

Air

The middle of a tunnel may be a long way from the open air. In the past, hundreds of workers used to die because there was no effective way of ventilating the tunnel. Things are better now. Wherever possible, engineers sink air shafts along the line of a tunnel to provide ventilation. It is even possible to sink them into the sea or a river bed by building towers that stick out of the water. These ensure that fresh air reaches every part of the tunnel, blowing away smoke and fumes and replacing stale air.

Ventilation experiment

You will need: two strong drinking straws, a thin cardboard tube, sticky tape, and some modeling clay.

1 Use the tape to close both ends of the cardboard tube.

2 Make two small holes in the top of the tube, side by side and a few inches apart, big enough for the straws to fit into.

3 Insert one drinking straw into each hole and seal the edges of the holes with clay so no air can escape. One is a ventilation shaft. The other is an exhaust shaft.

4 Blow down the ventilation shaft. What happens to the stale air in the tube? How does it leave the tunnel?

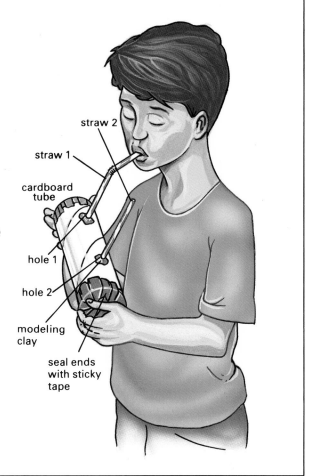

straw 2
straw 1
cardboard tube
hole 1
hole 2
modeling clay
seal ends with sticky tape

Tunnel maintenance

When the construction work on a tunnel is finished, there is still a lot of work to do before it is safe for people to use. Because car exhaust fumes are poisonous, providing good ventilation is essential in long road tunnels. Air **ducts** in the roof of the Great St. Bernard Road Tunnel, in Switzerland, are used to keep fresh air flowing. Fresh air coming in by one duct forces the stale air inside the tunnel into another duct, which takes it outside.

An American engineer named Clifford Milburn Holland solved the problem of underwater ventilation without air shafts. When he built the 1.7 mile (2.8 kilometer) Holland Tunnel under the Hudson River in New York, he put huge electric fans into buildings at each end of the tunnel to blow fresh air inside. They do the job so well that they change the air supply inside the tunnel every 90 seconds.

The fresh air flows through ducts under the traffic lanes. Holes in the ducts let the air into the tunnel. The fresh air forces the stale air and car fumes out through ducts in the roof.

Emergency!

Other safety systems must be put in place. There are spare fans that provide fresh air if the main ventilation system breaks down. There are fire and smoke alarms to give an early warning if fire breaks out. It can be very dangerous in a road tunnel if a car or truck catches fire. Most tunnels also have emergency telephones that drivers can use if their cars break down.

Accidents can still happen. The maintenance workers, who keep everything in working order, must be able to get their repair trucks to the scene of a breakdown quickly. Fire engines must be able to get through without delay. This is why service tunnels are built. The Channel Tunnel has a service tunnel in between the two main railway tunnels. The service tunnel will have smoke-proof doors. In an emergency, people will be able to leave the trains and get to safety through the service tunnel.

◀ There are huge fans at the top of these ventilation shafts in Hong Kong's Cross Harbor Tunnel. These help to keep the air circulating through the tunnel.

▲ Fire officers train to fight a tunnel fire. Tunnels pose many safety problems for the fire officers. They learn how to bring a dangerous fire under control quickly and safely.

▼ Large tunnels may have a control room. If there is an accident or a breakdown, it will show up on a screen. Rescue workers can be sent in without delay.

Tunnels in the future

Some time in the future, there may be tunnels linking the continents of North America and Asia or Europe and Africa. People may be able to travel by tunnel from Alaska to the USSR or from Spain to Morocco. Before such long tunnels can be built, however, engineers will have to discover better and cheaper ways of building them.

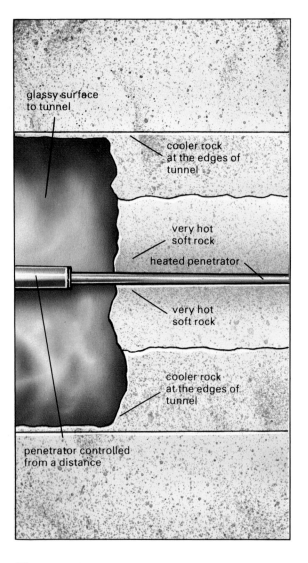

glassy surface to tunnel

cooler rock at the edges of tunnel

very hot soft rock

heated penetrator

very hot soft rock

cooler rock at the edges of tunnel

penetrator controlled from a distance

New machinery

Engineers are considering a new way of building a tunnel through hard rock. Some experts think that a long tunnel could be built with the aid of a **heated penetrator.**

To use a heated penetrator, the engineers would first drill a very deep hole in the rock face. Then they would insert the long needle of the penetrator into the hole. From a safe distance, the needle could be heated to a very high temperature.

The hard rock surrounding the needle would become soft and start to melt. Then machines would take the soft or liquid rock away. This method would produce a long tunnel the length of the penetrator. The rock on the roof and sides of this tunnel would cool slowly, forming a glassy surface that would line the tunnel as if it were concrete.

Planning and people

The tunnels of the future could make life much easier for the people who live in cities. Already, Montreal, in Canada, has a large number of tunnels connecting the basements of many of its shops. These tunnels make it easier for people shopping in the winter, when bad weather makes it hard to walk on the icy streets above. Perhaps the tunnels of the future will also be able to take high-speed roads and railways underground, so that the beauty of the countryside can remain unspoiled.

◀ Glass is made by heating sand and other minerals until they melt. Experts think that a heated penetrator could work in much the same way on rocks. Scientists have already begun to carry out experiments.

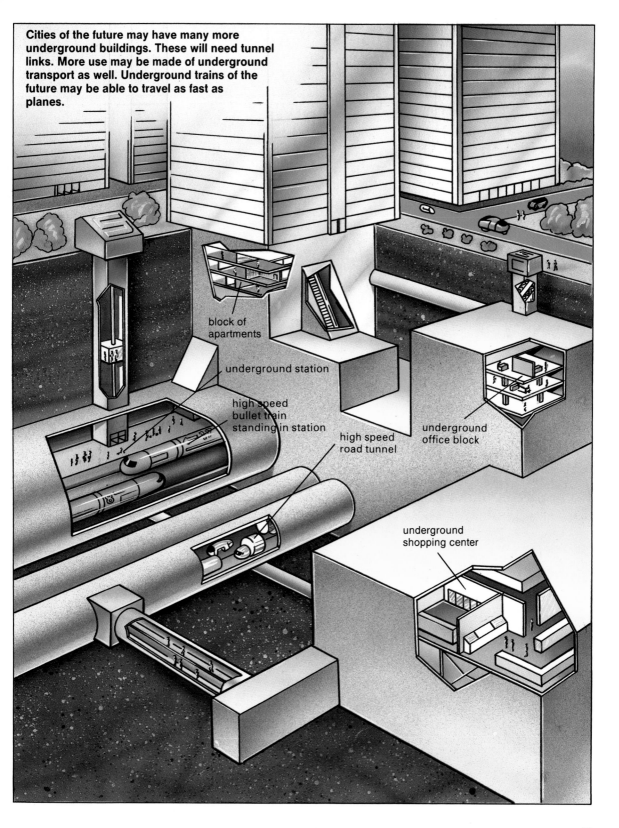

Cities of the future may have many more underground buildings. These will need tunnel links. More use may be made of underground transport as well. Underground trains of the future may be able to travel as fast as planes.

block of apartments

underground station

high speed bullet train standing in station

high speed road tunnel

underground office block

underground shopping center

Did you know?

* The longest road tunnel in the world is the 9.3 mile (16.4 kilometer) St. Gotthard Road Tunnel in Switzerland, which was opened in 1882.

* The longest underwater tunnel used by vehicles in the United States is the Bay Area Rapid Transit sunken-tube tunnel under San Francisco Bay. It is 3.6 miles (5.8 kilometers) long.

* The longest railway tunnels in the world are in Japan. The Oshimizu Tunnel, 13.8 miles (22.2 kilometers) long, was the longest tunnel until 1988, when it was surpassed by the Seikan Tunnel, which is 33.5 miles (53.8 kilometers) long.

* The longest railway tunnel in Europe is the Simplon Tunnel between Switzerland and Italy, which is 12.3 miles (19.8 kilometers) long. It was opened in 1922.

* Henderson Tunnel in Colorado is the longest railway tunnel in the United States. It is 9.8 miles (15.8 kilometers) long and was opened in 1975.

* The longest railway tunnel in New Zealand is the Rimutaka Tunnel. It is 5.5 miles (8.9 kilometers) long.

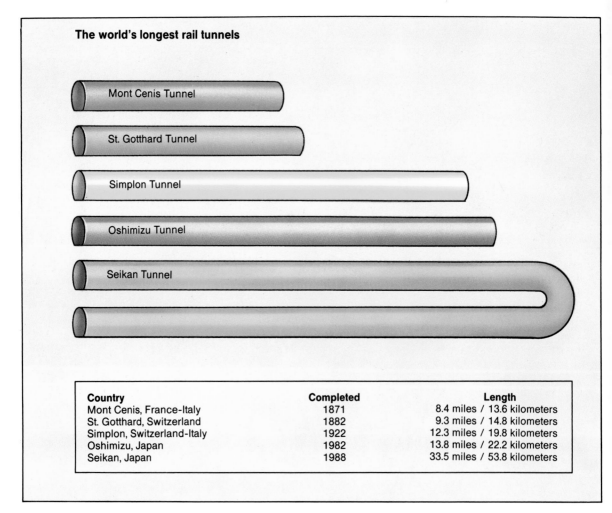

The world's longest rail tunnels

Mont Cenis Tunnel

St. Gotthard Tunnel

Simplon Tunnel

Oshimizu Tunnel

Seikan Tunnel

Country	Completed	Length
Mont Cenis, France-Italy	1871	8.4 miles / 13.6 kilometers
St. Gotthard, Switzerland	1882	9.3 miles / 14.8 kilometers
Simplon, Switzerland-Italy	1922	12.3 miles / 19.8 kilometers
Oshimizu, Japan	1982	13.8 miles / 22.2 kilometers
Seikan, Japan	1988	33.5 miles / 53.8 kilometers

▲ Modern tunneling methods have made the world a smaller place. Improved transport links have made travel much faster for all of us.

* The world's longest tunnel, 105 miles (169 kilometers) in length, is the Delaware Aqueduct. Completed in 1944, it pipes water from the Catskill Mountains into New York City.

* The fastest tunnel-boring machines in the world have been known to cut a tunnel through the ground at the rate of more than 328 feet (100 meters) a day.

* The longest sewage tunnel in the world is the 31 mile (50 kilometer) Central Outfall in Mexico City. Construction was completed in 1975.

* The longest rock tunnel taking water to a power station is the 16 mile (26 kilometer) Lochaber Tunnel in Scotland. It was opened in 1930.

Glossary

aqueduct: a structure, such as a tunnel or a bridge, which is built to carry flowing water from one place to another.

borehole: a hole drilled in the ground in order to obtain samples of rocks and soil from beneath the surface.

bulkhead: the steel plate at the end of a section of steel tube in a sunken tunnel.

compressed air: air that has been forced into a small space. In a tunneling shield, it prevents water from leaking into the tunnel workings.

conveyor belt: a moving belt used to carry objects from one place to another. In mines and tunnels, large conveyor belts may be used to move rocks or soil.

cut-and-cover tunnel: a tunnel built inside a ditch or trench in the ground and later covered over with earth.

detonator: any device, such as a fuse, that is used to set off an explosion.

dredge: to cut or hollow out a channel in the sea bed or the bed of a river.

drillbit: the cutting part of a machine used for drilling.

drill carriage: a wheeled truck with power drills in fixed positions.

drilling rig: a metal tower used to support the pipes used for drilling into the ground.

duct: a pipe or tube through which air or water can pass.

emery stone: a very hard mineral used for grinding and polishing.

engineer: a skilled person who designs machines, tunnels, roads, and bridges.

fault: a crack in the outer shell of the earth. Faults happen when the ground on one side of the crack is pushed up, sinks down, or moves sideways.

fold: a bend in layers of rock, caused by movements in the earth's outer shell.

front-end loader: a machine that can scoop up and transport large amounts of soil or rocks.

geologist: a scientist who studies the rocks that make up the earth.

grout: a thin cement used to fill cracks or to line shafts.

heated penetrator: a power tool, still in the experimental stage, that would bore through rock by melting it at very high temperatures.

hydraulic jack: a machine used to lift or move something very heavy, such as a tunneling shield.

hydroelectric power station: a building or buildings in which electric power is generated from fast-flowing water.

jumbo: a very large drill carriage that runs on wheels or tracks.

lining: a layer of material covering the inside of a tunnel. The material is usually concrete.

liquid nitrogen: the liquid form of a gas that can be used to freeze ground that is soaked with water.

mechanical mole: a popular name for the tunnel-boring machine.

roof bolt: a metal fixture that secures a steel mesh to the roof of a tunnel.

rotary excavator: a type of tunnel-boring machine.

settlement: a sinking movement of the land below the surface, which can cause damage to buildings on the ground above.

shaft: a deep hole in the ground. It is often dug to allow people to reach the tunnel workings or to let fresh air into the tunnel.

shotcrete: a liquid concrete that is sprayed onto tunnel walls by a machine.

stand-up time: the length of time that a tunnel roof can stay up without support.

sunken tube tunnel: a type of tunnel that is made when a steel tube is lowered onto the sea or river bed.

tunnel-boring machine: a powerful machine like a giant drill, which can be used to slice through rock to cut a tunnel.

tunneling shield: a large platform used to cut tunnels in soft rock. It shields the workers standing on it from roof falls.

turbine: a wheel with many curved blades that are turned by either water or gas. Turbines drive the machines that make electricity.

welding: joining two separate pieces of metal. The edges of both pieces are melted together.

Index